by Ezza Pickering

illustrated by Luke Jurevicius

www.HarcourtAchieve.com
1.800.531.5015

Characters

Lucas

Kanga

King Bouncy

Contents

Chapter 1

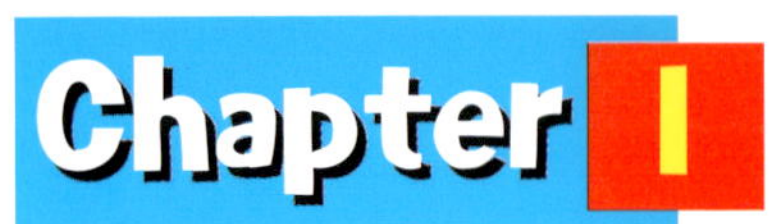

Time to Bounce

Lucas the Lizard likes to bounce. He bounces on bales of hay and herds of sheep.

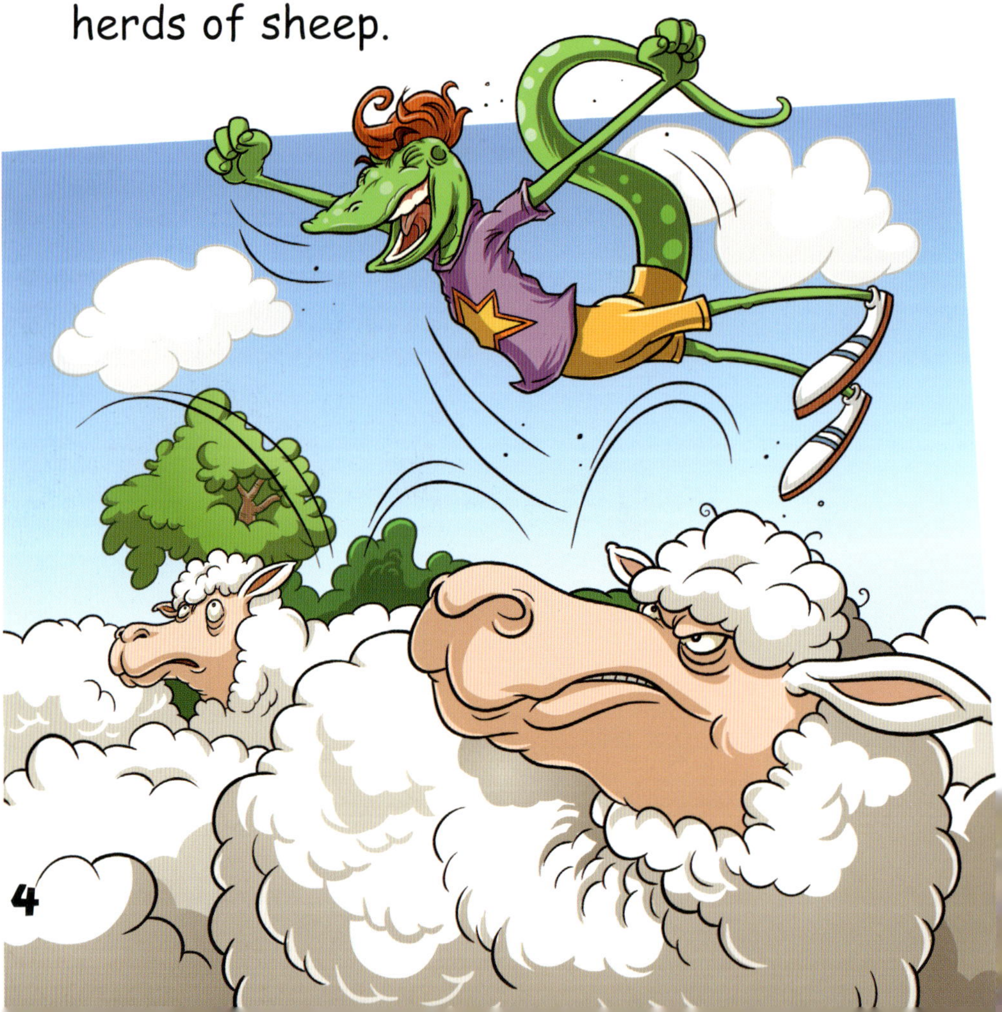

Most of all, he loves to bounce on trampolines. He thinks he is the best bouncer of all time.

“I’m the best in the world,” he shouts.
“Who could ever beat me?”

Lucas has a big head. It's time to put all his big talk to the test.

All the best jumpers enter. Hippo, Kanga, and Chuck the Chicken come early.

Someone is missing. Where is Lucas the Lizard?

A super-long car made of pure gold rolls up. Lucas the Lizard gets out of the car. Razzle-dazzle!

"I'm going to win this EASY!" he shouts to the crowd.

Chapter 2

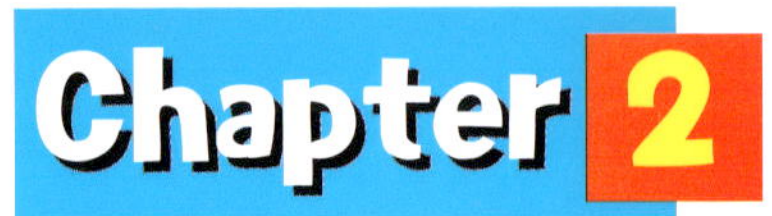

SPRIIIING!

Hippo goes first. As she jumps, the trampoline sinks lower and lower.

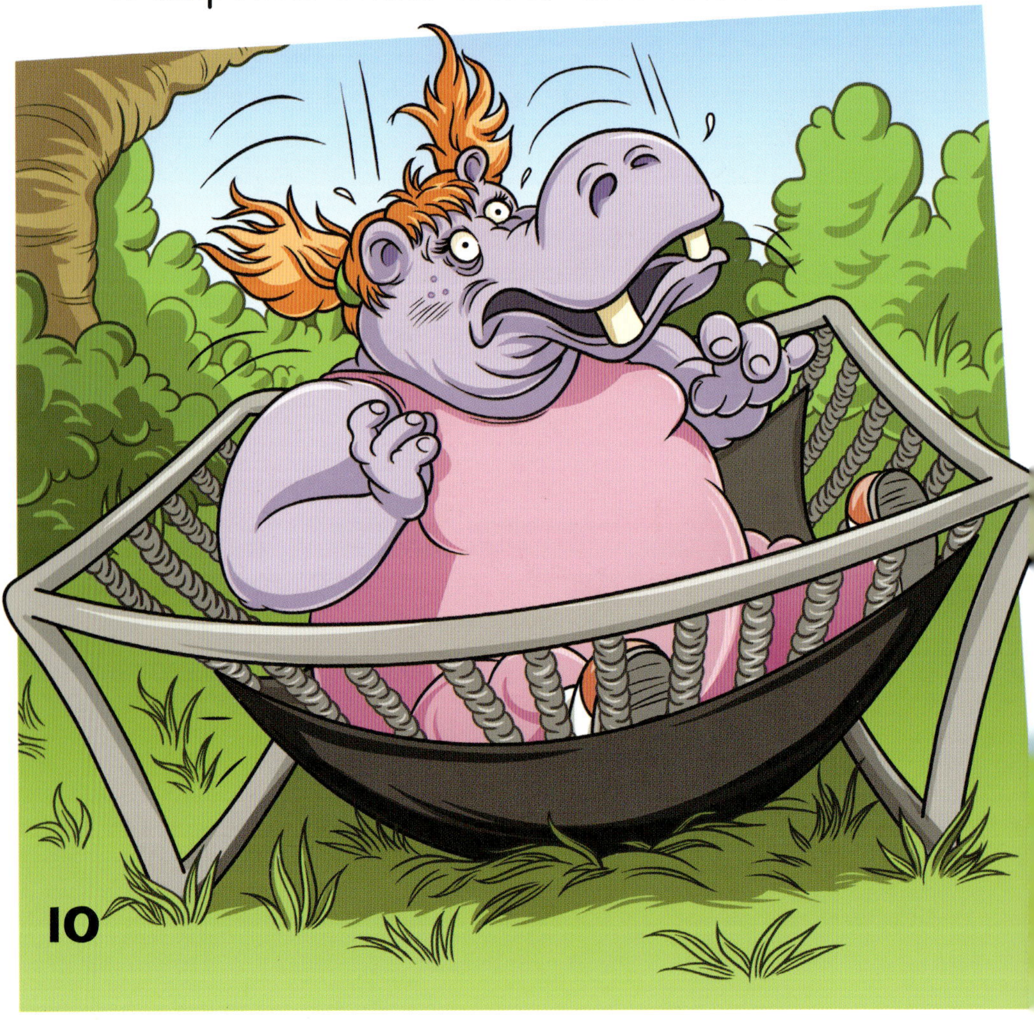

Chuck the Chicken cheats. He flaps his wings.

Kanga jumps so high, she touches a small cloud! She is sure to win.

Lucas just laughs.

"Ha! What a joke. I can jump higher in my sleep!"

It's true. Lucas jumps higher than everyone! He bounces so high, the crowd can't see him.

Lucas comes down for his final jump.

"Now you will all see why I am the best in the world!"

SPRIIIIIIING! Up and up and up Lucas flies. He watches stars and planets whiz past him.

Chapter 3

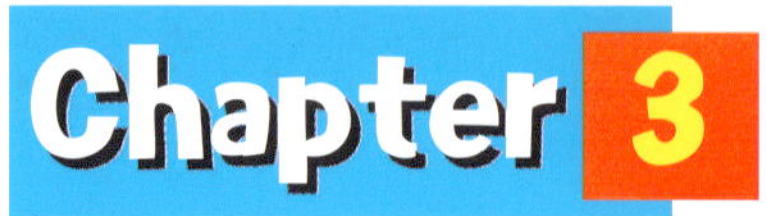

King Bouncy's Place

"Oh, no! I think that last bounce was too big."

He is headed straight for an ugly gray planet.

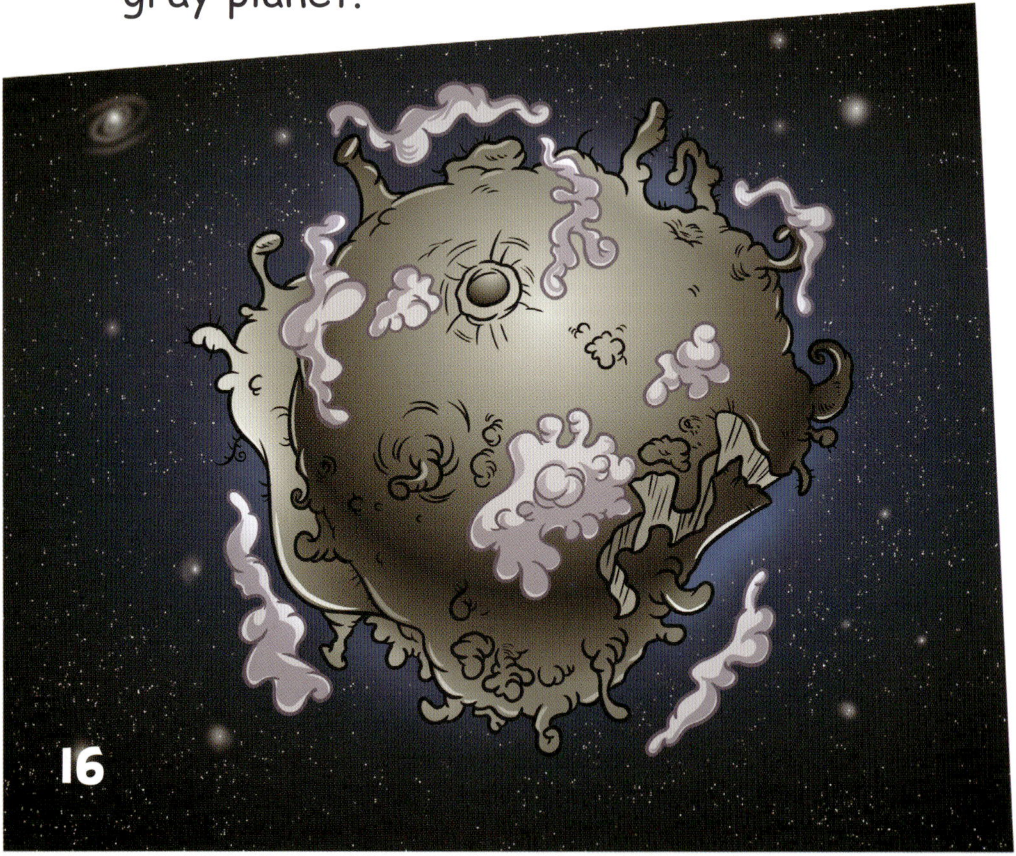

Lucas lands with a splat on top of a funny-looking tree.

Three large trampolines run straight for him. "You are in big trouble!" they all shout. The trampolines carry Lucas to a large palace.

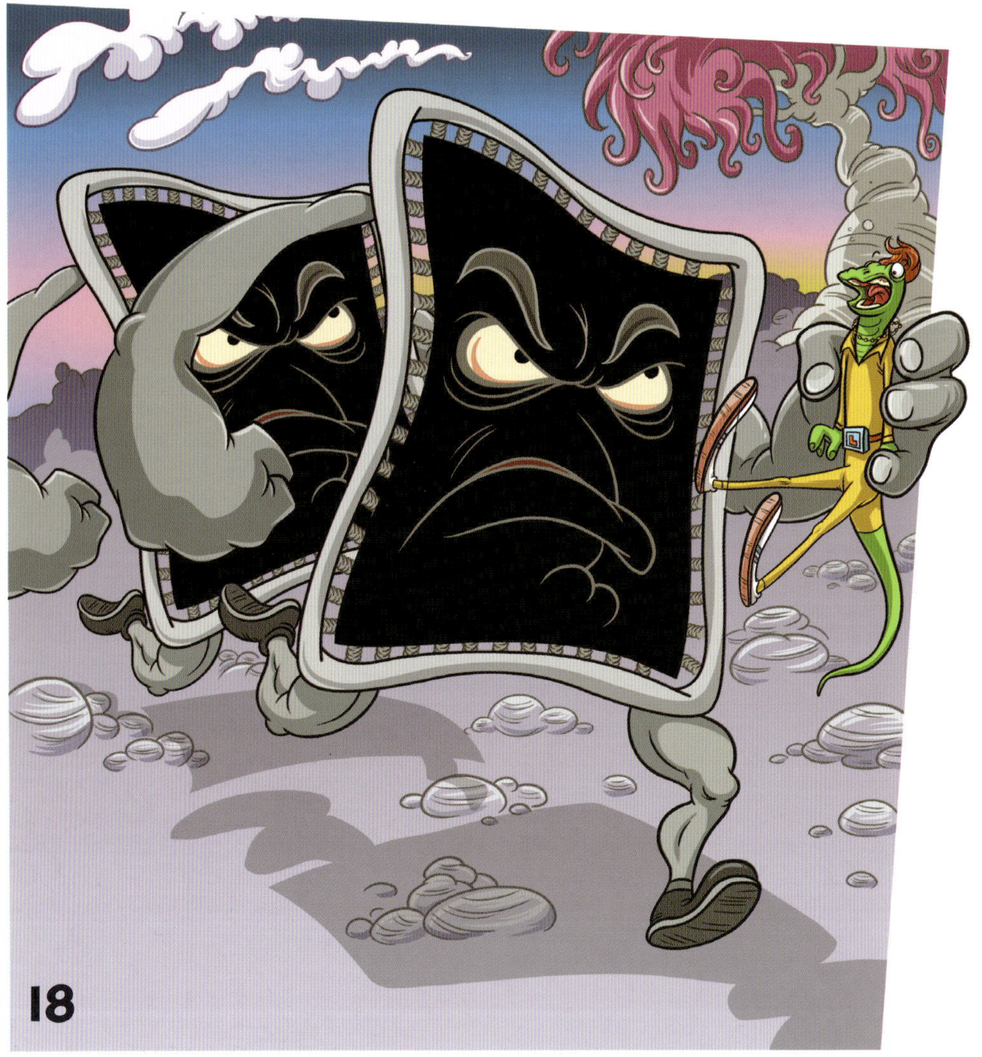

The gates creak open.

"What a huge trampoline. It's the largest I've ever seen," Lucas gasps.

"I am King Bouncy, and you are a nasty lizard. You hurt dear old Trampoline Boing."

"Isn't that what trampolines are for?" asks Lucas.

"NO! Trampolines are better than lizards," King Bouncy roars. "A trampoline should always be above a lizard."

Lucas hears a few groans. He looks down and sees four lizards. King Bouncy is sitting on them.

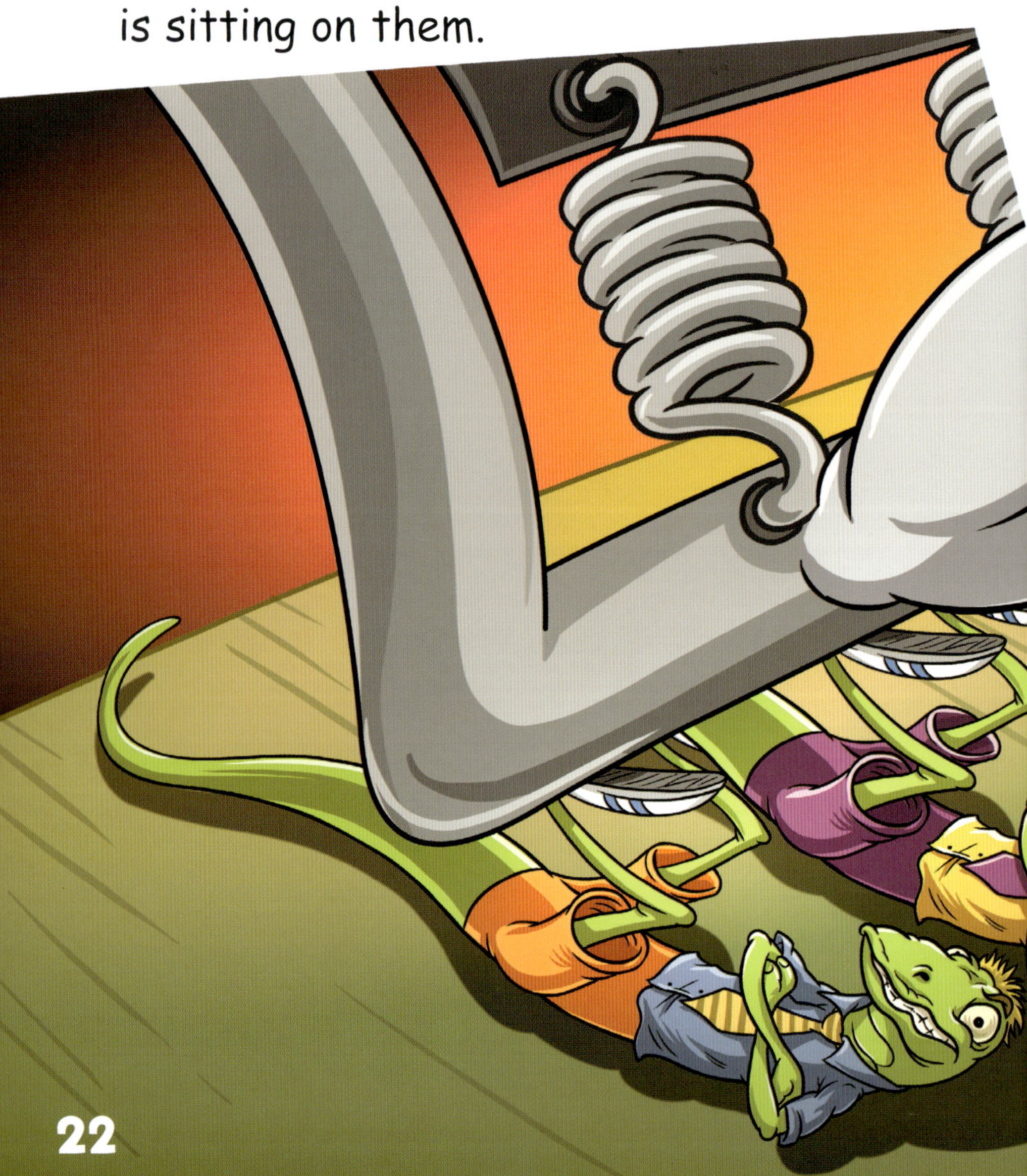

Suddenly another large trampoline bursts into the room. It is King Bouncy's daughter. "Daddy, Daddy, has my birthday present arrived? My poor feet are aching."

Chapter 4

The Winner

Lucas gasps. "I will not sit under her. I cannot! I will be crushed to death."

Lucas leaps with all his strength. Like a rocket, he flies out the palace window!

Lucas lands on the highest hill on the planet. He runs and jumps off the edge of the hill. "Yahooooo!"

He lands with a *boing* on a trampoline.
It's a sleepy trampoline cow.

Lucas flies back to Earth and lands with a *splash!* The crowd cheers. Lucas is the winner.

"I've seen where bouncing can take you. I've seen the highs and the lows." Lucas hands the trophy to Kanga. "My bouncing days are over."

Glossary

bales
tied up hay

cheats
acts unfairly

final
last time

gasps
a short, sharp breath

in my sleep

do something easily

planets

objects in space, like Earth

trampoline

a bouncy toy for jumping on

trophy

a prize given to winners

Ezza Pickering

Hi there. My name is Ezza Pickering, but I have to write quickly. You see I met Lucas the Lizard the other day and he was telling me how just one bounce on the sleepy cow trampoline returned him back to Earth. Wow! I wanted to try that. After all, I'm not a lizard, so I'd be safe on King Bouncy's planet, right? Wrong! I am writing this as I run into a live volcano to hide. You see, now the Cow Trampoline Police are after me . . . Oops, here they come . . . Oh, no, it's a stampeed . . . I'm out of here . . . *Lucas!*

Luke Jurevicius